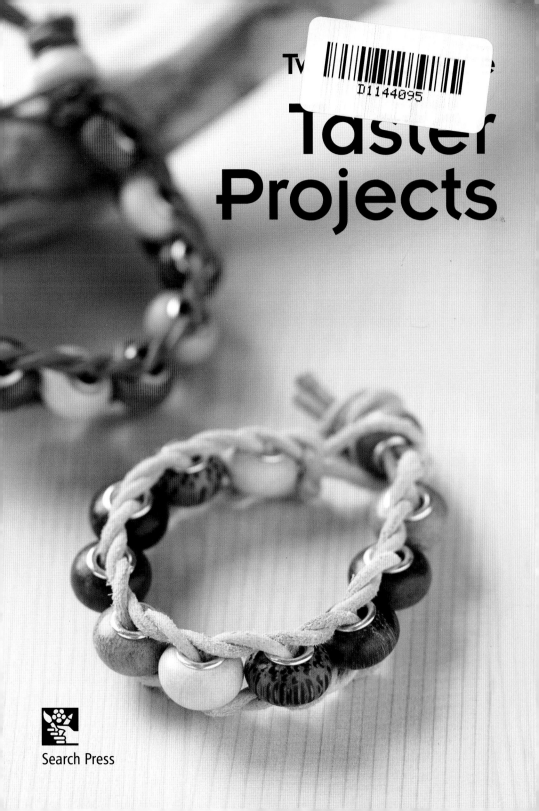

Taster
Projects

Search Press

First published in 2014

Search Press Limited
Wellwood, North Farm Road,
Tunbridge Wells, Kent TN2 3DR

Contains material from the following books in the Twenty to Make series by Search Press:

Mini Bunting by Alistair Macdonald, 2013
Sugar Dogs by Frances McNaughton, 2014
Crocheted Flowers by Jan Ollis, 2012
Mini Cross Stitch by Michael Powell, 2013
Knitted Mug Hugs by Val Pierce, 2010
Jelly Roll Scraps by Carolyn Forster, 2014
Crocheted Granny Squares by Val Pierce, 2012
Knitted Baby Bootees by Val Pierce, 2011
Sugar Animals by Frances McNaughton, 2009
Mini Christmas Crochet by Val Pierce, 2011
Stitched Fabric Brooches by Alex McQuade, 2014
Knitted Bears by Val Pierce, 2010
Button Jewellery by Marrianne Mercer, 2011
Felt Christmas Decorations by Corinne Lapierre, 2013
Crocheted Beanies by Frauke Kiedaisch, 2012
Friendship Bracelets by Pam Leach, 2014
Easy Knitted Scarves by Monica Russel, 2013
Steampunk Jewelllery by Carolyn Schulz, 2014
Sugar Wobblies by Georgie Godbold, 2013

Print ISBN: 978-1-78221-195-2

Suppliers
If you have difficulty in obtaining any of the materials and equipment mentioned in this book, then please visit the Search Press website for details of suppliers: www.searchpress.com

Printed in China

Contents

Introduction

This *Twenty to Make* book is a taster of 20 fantastic projects taken from a selection of fabulous *Twenty To Make* titles that have already been published.

We have included projects that use crafts such as knitting, crochet, sewing and stitching, cross stitch, sugarcraft, jewellery making and felt work, so that there is something for everyone to try. We hope that experimenting with these projects will inspire you to try out some of the *Twenty to Make* titles that these projects have been taken from, when you have had some fun making these tasters!

There are projects both for beginners and more experienced crafters to try; from stitching a simple but effective Christmas place setting in felt, and making a lovely pair of button earrings using pretty shell buttons; to crocheting a flower, or a gorgeous beanie hat, and trying your hand at sugarcraft, with a cute dog, a hippopotamus, or a fairy. You could also knit a scarf for the special person in your life, or a cute and cuddly teddy bear for a child. These exciting projects are sure to appeal to a wide range of crafters, and will make lovely gifts for family and friends alike.

Have fun and happy crafting!

20 Great Projects
taken from these fabulous titles

Mini Bunting — Alistair Macdonald

Sugar Dogs — Frances McNaughton

Crocheted Flowers — Jan Ollis

Mini Cross Stitch — Michael Powell

Knitted Mug Hugs — Val Pierce

Jelly Roll Scraps — Carolyn Forster

Crocheted Granny Squares — Val Pierce

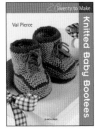

Knitted Baby Bootees — Val Pierce

Sugar Animals — Frances McNaughton

Mini Christmas Crochet — Val Pierce

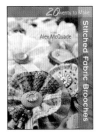

Stitched Fabric Brooches — Alex McQuade

Knitted Bears — Val Pierce

Button Jewellery — Marrianne Mercer

Felt Christmas Decorations

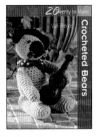

Crocheted Bears — Val Pierce

Modern Friendship Bracelets — Pam Leach

Easy Knitted Scarves — Monica Russel

Steampunk Jewellery — Catherine Schurz

Sugar Wobblies — Georgie Godbold

www.searchpress.com

Materials and tools

Christmas Bunting, page 8

Enlarging the template

To make a full-size template, simply enlarge the triangle, shown left, on a printer or photocopier to 200%. Use the template for both layers of fabric.

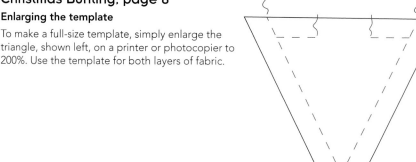

Simple Daisy, page 14

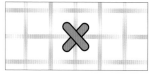

Cross stitch

How to work cross stitch, page 14

All cross stitch is worked in two strands except where indicated on the key. Each cross is made up of two stitches that together form an 'X'. The bottom stitch is worked from lower left to upper right, and the top stitch is worked from upper left to lower right.

Dog Brooch, page 28

Attaching a brooch finding

Cut a circle of fabric – appropriate to the size of the project – and stitch a brooch finding just above the centre point. Use strong thread that tones with the colour of your fabric, and hand sew through the finding's holes until it is secure. Then, either stitch the circular fabric to the rear of the project using blanket stitch – making sure that your stitching only catches the rear layer or layers of fabric and is not visible from the front of the brooch – or attach it using a glue gun.

Dog Brooch template, page 28, actual size

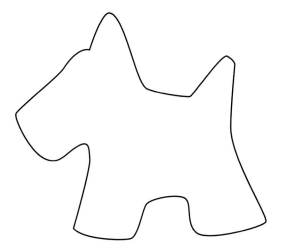

Seaside Shell Earrings, page 34
Use two pairs of pliers to open the jump ring.

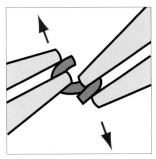

Sunflower Fairy, page 46

How to make the body

1 Roll 45g (1½oz) of modelling paste into a ball.
2 Shape the paste into a cone 6.5cm (2½in) tall.

3 Insert an 8cm (3¼in) cocktail stick through the middle of the cone to the base for support. The top of the cocktail stick will support the head. Make two holes in the front for the legs to fit in.

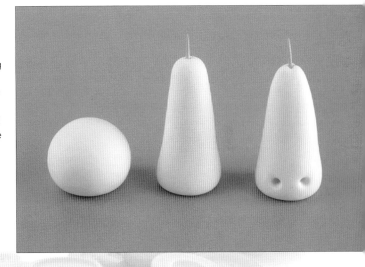

Christmas Bunting

Materials:

Card for template

Red and green floral fabric (I have used Liberty); 10 x 12cm (4 x 4¾in) per flag and the same to use as a lining

Large red jacket buttons

Red bias binding 2cm (¾in) wide, measure to the desired length of the bunting, plus ties at the ends

Green embroidery thread

Sewing thread to match the bias binding

Tools:

Pencil

Ruler

Fabric marker

Pins

Scissors, both paper and fabric

Iron

Sewing machine

Large upholstery needle or knitting needle

Hand sewing needle

Instructions:

1 Start by transferring the triangle template (page 6) on to card and cut it out.

2 With the fabric pinned right sides together, place the template on top and carefully draw around all of the edges using a fabric marker. Remove the template and secure the two layers together with pins, then cut round the marked lines. Repeat this process until you have enough flags for your bunting length.

3 Set a sewing machine to a medium-sized stitch. Take a flag and start to sew down one of the sides. Seam allowance has been added to the template at 1cm (³/₈in). As you reach the end of the first side, stop the stitching 1cm (³/₈in) away from the base of the work. Lift the foot and turn the flag towards you and continue stitching down the opposite edge. Now clip the excess fabric from the tip of the flag (see page 7) and turn right side out. Use the eye of a large upholstery or knitting needle to ease the tip of the flag out. Take care not to push too hard as this may result in the needle coming through the work. Press the flag flat and trim away the protruding seam allowance to maintain a straight edge along the top. Repeat this process until all of the flags have been completed.

8

4 Using an iron, carefully press the bias binding in half lengthwise, matching the edges together. Sandwich each flag between the folded bias and pin into position. Space evenly and alternate red flags with green flags; I have spaced mine 2.5cm (1in) apart. Make sure you leave enough free bias at the start and finish to allow for ties. Sew the bias binding together along the entire length using a sewing machine set to a medium straight stitch. Stitch as close to the edge as you can. Press the bunting flat.

5 Between each flag, hand sew a red jacket button in the centre of the bias binding using green embroidery thread.

Dachshund

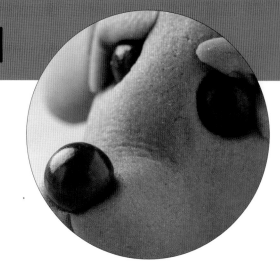

Materials:

20g (²/₃oz) chestnut modelling paste
Edible candy stick
Edible black sugar pearls

Tools:

2cm (¾in) oval cutter
Dresden tool
Water brush
Thin palette knife
Small, non-stick rolling pin

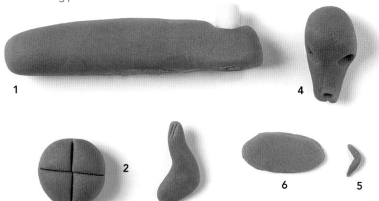

1

4

2

6

5

Instructions:

1 Shape 10g (¹/₃oz) of paste to a 6cm (2³/₈in) sausage for the body. Push a short candy stick vertically through the sausage at the neck end. Make a tiny short pointed cone for the tail and stick it on.

2 Cut 2g (¹/₁₂oz) of paste into four equal pieces for the legs. Roll each to form a 2cm (¾in) sausage. Curve each leg and mark toes with a knife.

3 Attach the legs to the sides of the body with all the toe ends pointing forwards.

4 Shape 2.5g (¹/₁₀oz) paste to a long pear shape. Shape the fat end of the head to form a higher forehead. Mark the eyes and nose with a Dresden tool. Insert edible black sugar pearls for the eyes and nose. Mark the mouth using a knife.

5 Make two very tiny sausages of paste and attach over the eyes.

6 Roll out the paste thinly and cut out two small oval shapes for ears. Attach them to the top of the head facing backwards, and then fold them over to look floppy, as shown.

Twenty to Make

Frances
McNaughton

Sugar Dogs

Pink Cosmos

Materials and equipment:

No. 3 crochet cotton in lime green, pale green and bright pink

Crochet hook size 3.00mm (US D-0, UK 11)

Bodkin or large-eyed needle for sewing in the ends

Instructions:

With lime green crochet cotton, make
a slip ring.

Round 1: 2 ch, sc (*UK dc*) into ring 8 times. Fasten off the lime green crochet cotton.

Change to pale green and ss together.

Round 2: 2 ch, hdc (*UK htr*) into each sc (*UK dc*) 8 times, 1 hdc (*UK htr*) into base ch of 2 ch, join in bright pink and ss into 2 ch.

Make the petal cluster:

*2 ch, 1 dc (*UK tr*), 1 tr (*UK dtr*), 1 dc (*UK tr*), 2 ch, ss, all into first ch of 2 ch, hdc (*UK htr*), sc (*UK dc*) into next hdc (*UK htr*)*, repeat from * to * 8 more times (making 9 petals in total).

Tie off and sew in the ends.

*These lovely little flowers
work in all sorts of colour
combinations. Use them
to decorate cushions,
lampshades and throws
around the home.*

12

Simple Daisy

Colour key:

L	Navy Blue ultra vy lt (129)
ℓ	Tangerine lt (313)
1	Pink vy lt (48)
A	Topaz ultra vy lt (305)
r	White bright + Pink vy lt (1 + 48)
Y	White bright + Lavender lt (1 + 108)
(	White bright (1)
~	Dusty Violet vy lt (103)

Stitching notes:

Stitch count: 20 x 20.

Design area: 3.6 x 3.6cm (1½ x 1½in) at 55sts per 10cm (4in).

Where two colours are shown against a symbol, use one strand of each colour.

See page 6 for how to work cross stitch.

Outlines

All of the outlines are in long stitch with one strand of Black (403).

Fabric preparation

The designs in this book were stitched on 14 count Aida fabric. Other fabrics such as evenweave and canvas can be used as an alternative. On occasion, your fabric can fray slightly round the edges. You can prevent this by oversewing or placing masking tape over the raw edges.

Anchor embroidery thread is used here, and the numbers accompanying the colour keys refer to this brand's threads. If you use a different brand of thread, such as DMC or Madeira, then conversion charts are readily available.

Before you start stitching, find the centre of your fabric by folding it in half lengthways and widthways, and mark the centre with a pin. The centre of the design can be found on the chart opposite by following the arrows on each side, top and bottom. Mark the centre of the chart and begin stitching at the centre of the design.

Reading the charts

One symbol on a square represents one full cross stitch worked in the colour specified. One full stitch on Aida is worked over one square, while on evenweave it is worked over two threads.

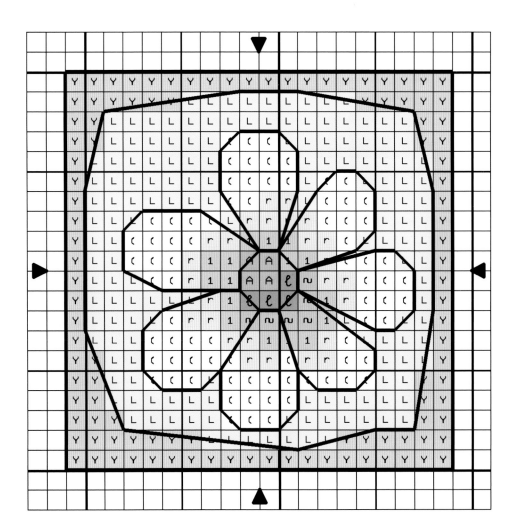

Getting started

You will need a tapestry needle in size 24 or 26. This is a special blunt needle that will not split your stitches.

To secure the thread, use the loop method: fold one strand of thread in half, then thread the two ends through the needle. Take the needle up through the fabric at the given point and work the first half of the cross, being careful not to pull the thread right through. Before completing the second half of the stitch pass the needle through the loop of the thread at the back of the work.

Time for Tea

Materials:

1 ball red double knitting yarn

Oddments of 4-ply yarn in pale turquoise and green

3 pink flower buttons

Needles:

1 pair 4.00mm (UK 8; US 6) and 1 pair 3.25mm (UK 10; US 3) knitting needles

Instructions:

Using 4.00mm (UK 8; US 6) needles and red yarn, cast on 7 sts.

Knit 2 rows. Continue in GS.

Inc 1 st at each end of next and every alt row until 17 sts on needle.

Work 64 rows in GS.

Dec 1 st at each end of next and every alt row until 11 sts rem.

Next row: to make the buttonhole, K2tog, K3, yrn twice, K2tog, K2, K2tog.

Next row: knit, dropping the yrn of previous row and knitting into the loops.

Continue to dec until 7 sts rem.

Work 2 rows in GS.

Cast off.

Tea bag:

Using 3.25mm (UK 10; US 3) needles and turquoise yarn, cast on 13 sts.

Work 22 rows in GS.

Next row: cast off 5 sts, knit to end.

Next row: cast off 5 sts, knit to end.

Work 6cm (2¼in) in GS on rem 3 sts. Cast off.

Leaf:

Using 3.25mm (UK 10; US 3) needles and green yarn, cast on 3 sts.

Knit 2 rows.

Inc 1 st at each end of next and every alt row until 7 sts on needle.

Work 2 rows in GS.

Next row: K2tog at each end of row.

Next row: K1, sl1, K2tog, psso, K1.

Next row: K1, K2tog.

Next row: K2tog. Fasten off.

To make up:

Work in all ends neatly. Sew two buttons and the leaf on to the centre of the tea bag. Attach the tea bag by stitching the top of the cord to the back of the mug cosy. Sew on the remaining button to correspond with the buttonhole.

Give these simple designs a personal touch to make a special gift for a friend or relative. For example, add buttons or motifs to the teabag that reflect their favourite colours, pets, hobbies or interests.

Itsy Bitsy Bag

Materials:

9 x 2½in (6.5cm) squares of light-coloured fabric

9 x 2½in (6.5cm) squares of dark-coloured fabric

1 Jelly Roll strip for the gusset, 2½ x 22in (6.5 x 56cm)

Lining fabric, 12 x 7¼in (30.5 x 18.5cm)

Fabric for loop, 2½ x 3in (6.5 x 7.5cm) cut in half lengthways to make a strip 1¼in (3.25cm) wide

Fabric for handles, 2½ x 22in (6.5 x 56cm)

Button for closure, 1in (2.5cm) diameter

Tools:

Basic sewing kit

Scissors

Sewing machine

Rotary cutting mat, ruler and cutter (optional)

Pen to mark fabric

Iron and ironing mat

Finished size:

7 x 7in (18 x 18cm) excluding handles

Instructions:

1 On the back of the light squares, draw a diagonal line from corner to corner. Place these on top of the dark squares, right sides facing. Stitch along either side of the line, ¼in (0.5cm) away from the line.

2 Cut the squares in half along the drawn line and press the seams open. You will have 18 of these in total.

3 Lay nine of the squares out in three rows of three, with all the seams running in the same direction. Sew the squares together in rows, pressing the seams in alternating directions on each row. Sew the rows together to make a block. Press the seams open. Make two of these blocks, one for each side of the bag.

4 Stitch the gusset around three sides of one of the blocks, right sides facing. Press the seams towards the gusset. Repeat, sewing the other block to the gusset. Press the seams towards the gusset.

5 To make the loop for the button fastening, fold the fabric in half lengthways, wrong sides together, and fold the raw edges into the fold. Press and machine stitch along the edge.

6 Fold the strip in half to form a loop and pin it centrally on the back of the bag on the wrong side, just below the top edge. The loop should be pointing downwards into the bag.

7 Now make two handles. Fold the piece of fabric for the handles in half lengthways, wrong sides together, and fold the edges into the middle as you did for the loop. Press and machine stitch along each edge to secure.

8 Cut the fabric in half widthways to make two handles. Pin these on the top edge of the bag, one on each side. Align the raw edges and position them in the middle of the two outside squares. The handles will be facing down into the bag.

9 To make the lining, fold the lining fabric right sides together so that it measures 6 x 7¼in (15 x 18.5cm) and machine up each side. On one side leave a 2in (5cm) gap in the middle for turning through later.

10 To shape the lining base, refold the lining so that the seams are in the middle and mark 1in (2.5cm) on either side of one of the seams across the point. Stitch across between these two marks. Secure the stitching and cut off the point leaving ¼in (0.5cm) seam allowance. Repeat for the second seam.

11 Place the outer bag inside the lining, right sides together. Match the side seams and pin. Sew around the top of the bag.

12 Turn the bag right-side out, sew the opening in the lining closed and press.

13 Sew the button on the bag about ½in (1cm) down from the top edge.

Daffodil Square

Materials and equipment:

Crochet hook size 3.00mm (US D; UK 10)

DMC Petra 3 crochet cotton – small amounts in each of 4 colours: A, B, C and D. Alternatively, 1 x 50g ball in each colour will make several squares.

Motif size:

3in (7.5cm) diameter

Instructions:

Using A, 8 ch, join with a sl st into a circle.

Round 1: 1 ch, work 16 sc (*UKdc*) into ring, join as before. Break A.

Round 2: using B, 3 ch, 2 dc (*UKtr*) into same st, leaving last loop of each dc (*UKtr*) on hook, yrh and draw yarn through all loops on hook, *2 ch, miss 1 sc (*UKdc*), 3 dc (*UKtr*) into next sc (*UKdc*) leaving last loop of each st on hook, yrh, draw yarn through all loops*, rep from * to * all round, ending last rep with 2 ch, miss 1 sc (*UKdc*), sl st to top of 3 ch at beg of round. Break B.

Round 3: using C, sl st into first 2 ch sp, 3 ch, 3 dc (*UKtr*) into same sp, *3 ch, 4 dc (*UKtr*) into next 2 ch sp*, rep from * to * all round, ending last rep with 3 ch, join with a sl st to top of 3 ch at beg of round. Break C.

Round 4: sl st to first 3 ch sp. Using D, [3 ch, 4 dc (*UKtr*), 2 ch, 5 dc (*UKtr*)] into same sp, *4 dc (*UKtr*) into next sp, [5 dc (*UKtr*), 2 ch, 5 dc (*UKtr*)] into next sp*, rep from * to * all round, sl st to top of 3 ch at beg of round. Fasten off and work in all the ends.

Simply Blue

Materials:

1 x 50g ball 4-ply baby yarn in blue

Needles:

1 pair 3.75mm (UK 9; US 5) knitting needles

Instructions:

Make two.

Cast on 37 sts.
Row 1: knit.
Row 2: K1, *inc in next st, K15, inc in next st*, K1, rep from * to * once more, K1.
Row 3: knit.
Row 4: K2, *inc in next st, K15, inc in next st*, K3, rep from * to *, K2.
Row 5: knit.
Row 6: K3, *inc in next st, K15, inc in next st*, K5, rep from * to *, K3.
Row 7: knit.
Row 8: K4, *inc in next st, K15, inc in next st,* K7, rep from * to *, K4.
Row 9: knit.
Row 10: K5, *inc in next st, K15, inc in next st*, K9, rep from * to *, K5.
Row 11: knit.
Work ridge pattern as follows:
Row 12: knit.
Row 13: purl.
Row 14: knit.
Row 15: knit.
Row 16: purl.
Row 17: knit.

Rep rows 12–17 once.
Shape instep as follows:
Row 1: K33, sl1, K1, psso, turn.
Row 2: sl1, K9, P2tog, turn.
Row 3: sl1, K9, sl1, K1, psso, turn.
Rep rows 2 and 3 eight times.
Rep row 2.
Next row: knit.
Work 3 more rows in GS, decreasing 1 st in centre of last row.
Work twisted rib as follows:
Next row: *K1tbl, P1*, rep from * to *.
Rep row 1 twenty times, cast off in rib.

To make up the bootees

Sew up the foot and back seams neatly. Turn over the ribbed top to form a cuff.

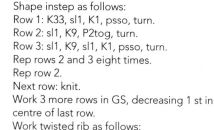

Hippopotamus

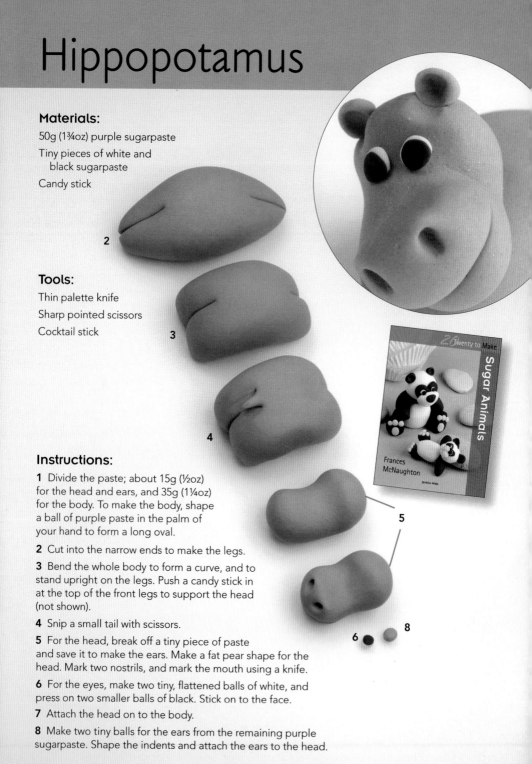

Materials:

50g (1¾oz) purple sugarpaste

Tiny pieces of white and black sugarpaste

Candy stick

Tools:

Thin palette knife

Sharp pointed scissors

Cocktail stick

Instructions:

1 Divide the paste; about 15g (½oz) for the head and ears, and 35g (1¼oz) for the body. To make the body, shape a ball of purple paste in the palm of your hand to form a long oval.

2 Cut into the narrow ends to make the legs.

3 Bend the whole body to form a curve, and to stand upright on the legs. Push a candy stick in at the top of the front legs to support the head (not shown).

4 Snip a small tail with scissors.

5 For the head, break off a tiny piece of paste and save it to make the ears. Make a fat pear shape for the head. Mark two nostrils, and mark the mouth using a knife.

6 For the eyes, make two tiny, flattened balls of white, and press on two smaller balls of black. Stick on to the face.

7 Attach the head on to the body.

8 Make two tiny balls for the ears from the remaining purple sugarpaste. Shape the indents and attach the ears to the head.

24

Make a baby hippopotamus by reducing all the sizes and using pink sugarpaste.

Christmas Cracker

Materials and equipment:

Crochet hook size 2.00mm (US B-1, UK 14)

No. 5 crochet cotton – 1 ball of green and 1 ball of red

1m (40in) of narrow red satin ribbon

0.5m (20in) of gold ric-rac braid

1 gold rose embellishment

Small piece of card

Small amount of stuffing

Sewing needle and thread to match the yarns

Measurements:

The cracker is approximately 14cm (5½in) long.

Instructions:

Using green crochet cotton, make 27 ch.
Row 1: work 1 dc (*UKtr*) into 3rd ch from hook, 1 dc (*UKtr*) into each ch to end, turn.
Row 2: 1 ch, work 1 sc (*UKdc*) into each dc (*UKtr*) to end, turn.
Row 3: 3 ch, miss first st, work 1 dc (*UKtr*) into each sc (*UKdc*) to end, turn.
Row 4: repeat row 2.

Change to red cotton.
Rows 5–14: repeat rows 3 and 4 five times.

Change to green cotton.
Rows 15–18: repeat rows 3 and 4 twice.
Fasten off.

To make up

Work in the ends. Fold the crochet lengthways to form a tube and then sew the long edges together, matching the colours and rows. The seam will be on the underside of the piece.

Measure a piece of card slightly shorter than the inner red section of the cracker. Roll it into a tube then try the tube inside the crochet to get a good fit. When you are happy with the size, glue the edges of the card together and slip the tube inside the cracker.

Add some stuffing to the inside of the tube to give the cracker more body. Cut the red ribbon into two lengths and tie one tightly to each end of the cracker either side of the tube section, using the photograph as a guide. Trim the ribbon if necessary for a smart finish. Measure a piece of gold ric-rac braid long enough to fit around the central red section and glue it in place with the join on the underside. Glue the gold rose embellishment to the centre as shown in the photograph.

> **Tip**
> Hide the join on the ric-rac braid under the rose embellishment for a super-neat finish.

Dog Brooch

Materials:
Dog-coloured felt
Embroidery thread
Polyester filling
Ribbon
Button
Brooch finding

Tools:
Fabric scissors
Embroidery needle

Instructions:

1 Using the template on page 7, cut out two dog body shapes from the coloured felt.

2 Lay one piece on top of the other, aligning them perfectly, and secure them in the centre with a pin.

3 Starting at the top of the tail and moving anti-clockwise, hand sew a blanket stitch around the outer edge. Pause when you reach the bottom of the dog's back leg. Remove the pin.

4 Stuff the shape with a little polyester filling and continue the blanket stitch until the dog is stitched closed.

5 Cut a length of ribbon 12.5cm (5in) long and cut one end at a sharp diagonal angle. Thread the button onto the ribbon.

6 Place the ribbon around the dog's neck and secure it at the back with a double knot. Cut off any excess ribbon, snipping the ends at an angle to prevent them from fraying.

7 Attach the brooch finding (see page 6).

Tip: filling your dog
Use a knitting needle or pencil to insert the polyester wadding; use only very small amounts at a time and you will fill the shape more evenly.

Personalised pooch
Try using different colours and button shapes to change the look and personalise the brooch. Or try adding a bell to create a lovely festive brooch for Christmas time!

Basic Bear

Bear:

Materials
1 ball double knitting yarn

Small quantity of soft textured, high quality safety stuffing

2 x 6mm round black beads for eyes

Black embroidery thread or floss for features

Sewing needles

Stitch holder

Needles
1 pair 3.25mm (UK 10; US 3) knitting needles

Instructions

Work entirely in GS, unless otherwise stated.

Head
Cast on 30 sts.
Rows 1–4: GS.
Row 5: K2, skpo, knit to last 3 sts, K2tog, K1.
Rows 6–7: GS.
Continue to dec in this way on every third row until 8 sts rem.
Next row: K2, skpo, K2tog, K2.
Next row: K2, skpo, K2.
Next row: K1, sl1, K2tog, psso, K1.
Next row: K3tog.
Fasten off.

Body and legs (make two pieces the same)
Cast on 12 sts.
Rows 1–2: GS.
Rows 3–8: inc 1 st at each end of rows 3, 5 and 7 [18 sts].
Rows 8–33: knit.
Row 34: divide for legs. K8, cast-off 2, knit to end [8 sts].
Proceed on these 8 sts for first leg.
Rows 35–52: knit.
Row 53: K2tog, knit to last 2 sts, K2tog.
Row 54: cast off.

Return to stitches left on needle, rejoin yarn and complete to match first leg.

Arms (make two)
Cast on 6 sts.
Row 1: knit.
Row 2: knit twice into each st to end [12 sts].
Rows 3–6: knit.
Row 7: inc 1 st at each end of row [14 sts].
Rows 8–27: knit.
Rows 28–30: dec 1 st at each end of rows 28 and 30 [10 sts].
Row 31: K2, (K2tog) 3 times, K2 [7 sts].
Row 32: knit.
Cast off (this is the top of the arm).

Making up
1. Make up the head by folding the three corners of the triangle into the centre; the fold lines are shown in the top diagram above right. Sew the two side seams either side of the nose, and across the corner lines to form the ears, as shown in the lower diagram above right.

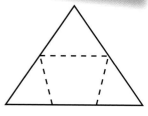

2. Sew a little way along the neck seam, just down from the nose. Stuff the head firmly to give it a good shape. Stitch on the nose and mouth with black thread, and sew on the eyes.

3. Stitch the back and front body pieces together using a flat seam on the right side of the work. Leave the neck edge open for stuffing. Stuff firmly and then close the neck opening. Attach the head to the body.

Shoes (make two):

Using an appropriate colour and 3.25mm (UK 10; US 3) needles, cast on 14 sts.
Next row: knit.
Next row: inc in each st across row [28 sts].
Work 5 rows GS.
Next row: K2tog, K8, (K2tog) 4 times, K8, K2tog.
Next row: K9, (K2tog) twice, K9.
Next row: knit.
Cast off. Stitch the seam along the base and back of the shoe. Put a tiny amount of stuffing inside the shoe, place the base of the leg inside the shoe and stitch it in place. Add embellishments.

Trousers (make two pieces the same):

Using an appropriate colour and 3.25mm (UK 10; US 3) needles, cast on 13 sts.
Rows 1–4: GS.
Rows 5–20: SS, ending on a purl row. Break yarn and leave these 13 sts on a spare needle.
Now work another piece to match. Do not break off yarn but continue as follows:
Knit across 13 sts on needle, cast on 2 sts, work across 13 sts left on spare needle [28 sts].
Next row: purl.

*Work a further 2 rows in SS, ending on a purl row.
Next row: K2, skpo, knit to last 4 sts, K2tog, K2.
Next row: purl.*
Repeat from * to * [24 sts].
Work 4 rows in rib, or as given in instructions.

Dress:

Bodice front
Cast on 24 sts.
Rows 1–6: SS.
Rows 7–8: cast off 2 sts at beg of each row.
Rows 9–10: SS.
Row 11: dec 1 st at each end of row [18 sts].
Row 12: purl.
Rows 13–16: SS.

Divide for neck
Work 7 sts, slip next 4 sts on to stitch holder, work 7 sts.
Continue on first 7 sts for side of neck.
Dec 1 st at neck edge on next and following alt rows until 4 sts rem.
Cast off.
Work other side to match.

Bodice back
Work rows 1–16 of bodice front.
Rows 17–21: SS.
Cast off.

Skirt
With RS facing, pick up and knit 24 sts along cast-on edge of bodice front.
Next row: purl.
Next row: knit twice into each st [48 sts].
Continue in SS and complete as given in pattern.
Repeat the above, on bodice back.

Neckband
Join one shoulder seam.
With RS facing, pick up and knit 5 sts down one side of neck, 4 sts from stitch holder

across front of neck, 5 sts up other side of neck and 10 sts around back of neck (rem 4 sts will form other shoulder).
Next row: knit.
Cast off knitwise.

Toby Toddler Bear

Materials

1 ball denim blue double knitting

Oddments of turquoise, green and orange yarn

Black embroidery thread

Small candy cane button

Small amount of safety stuffing

Materials for basic bear, including beige double knitting

Needles:

1 pair 3.25mm (UK 10; US 3) knitting needles

Instructions:

Make the basic bear (see page 6).

Dungarees

Front:

Using denim blue, cast on 13 sts.

Rows 1–4: GS.

Rows 5–20: SS, ending on a purl row. Break yarn and leave these 13 sts on a spare needle. Now work another piece to match. Do not break off yarn but continue as follows:

Row 21: knit across 13 sts on needle, cast on 2 sts, work across 13 sts left on spare needle [28 sts].

Row 22: purl.

Rows 23–24: SS, ending on a purl row.

Row 25: K2, skpo, knit to last 4 sts, K2tog, K2.

Row 26: purl.

Rows 27–30: repeat rows 23–26 [24 sts].

Rows 31–34: GS.

Bib:

Row 35: (RS facing) cast off 8 sts (1 st left on needle), knit a further 7 sts, cast off rem 8 sts. Turn and continue to work on rem 8 sts.

Row 36: (WS facing) K2, P4, K2.

Row 37: knit.

Rows 38–41: repeat rows 36–37 twice.

Row 42: as row 36.

Rows 43–46: GS.

Row 47: K2, cast off 4 sts, K2.

Working on first set of 2 sts for straps, continue in GS until strap fits over shoulder and down to waist on back of bear. Cast off.

Return to other set of 2 sts and make a second strap to match. Cast off.

Back:

Work as front of dungarees (rows 1–34). Cast off.

Patch:

Using a colour of your choice, cast on 6 sts. Work 10 rows in GS. Cast off.

Ball

Using turquoise, cast on 6 sts.

Row 1: purl.

Row 2: inc in each st across row [12 sts].

Row 3: purl.

Row 4: (K1, inc in next st) across row [18 sts].

Row 5: purl.

Row 6: (K2, inc in next st) across row [24 sts].

Row 7: purl.

Rows 8–9: SS.

Break yarn.

Change to orange yarn.

Rows 10–13: GS, beg with a knit row.

Break yarn and join in green yarn.

Rows 14–15: SS, ending with purl row.

Row 16: (K2, K2tog) across row [18 sts].

Row 17: purl.

Row 18: (K1, K2tog) across row [12 sts].

Row 19: purl.

Row 20: K2tog across row [6 sts].

Row 21: purl.

Break yarn and run end through rem sts. Pull up tight and secure.

Making up

Sew the seams of the dungarees, slip them on to the bear, cross the straps behind the bear's head and secure them on the back waistband. Place the patch on the dungaree knee (as shown in the photograph) and stitch it in place using large stitches. For the ball, Sew the side seam, and stuff the ball to give a rounded shape before closing. Sew the candy cane button inside the waistband.

Seaside Shell Earrings

Materials:

8 x 10mm (³⁄₈in) silver-plated jump rings

4 x 5mm (³⁄₁₆in) silver-plated jump rings

2 x 4cm (1⁵⁄₈in) silver-plated chain

2 x silver-plated earring hooks

4 x 18mm (¾in) shell buttons

2 x 15mm (⁵⁄₈in) turquoise buttons

Tools:

Flat-nosed pliers

Wire cutters

Snipe (chain)-nosed pliers

Scissors

Beading mat

Ruler

Instructions:

1 Attach a 10mm (³⁄₈in) jump ring through one of the holes in a shell button (see diagram on page 7). Attach to this a 5mm (³⁄₁₆in) jump ring, and then an earring finding on to that.

2 Add another 10mm (³⁄₈in) jump ring through the other hole in the same button and attach to that a 5mm (³⁄₁₆in) jump ring and a 4cm (1⁵⁄₈in) length of chain.

3 On the other end of the chain attach another shell button with a 10mm (³⁄₈in) jump ring.

4 Now use another 10mm (³⁄₈in) jump ring to attach a turquoise button around one-third of the way down the chain so that it hangs centrally between the two shell buttons.

5 Repeat all the above steps for the second earring.

Bronzed Beauty

Warm to the seaside theme by using bronze-coloured shell buttons with wooden buttons and gold chain.

Christmas Place Setting

Materials:

25 x 15cm (9¾ x 6in) of grey felt

10 x 10cm (4 x 4in) of white felt

60cm (23½in) of red ric-rac

Red embroidery cotton

Tools:

Paper, fabric and embroidery scissors

Zigzag scissors

Dressmaking pins

Embroidery needle

Pencil, ruler and pair of compasses

Paper

Fabric glue

Instructions:

1 On your piece of paper draw a 10 x 15cm (4 x 6in) rectangle, a 15 x 5cm (6 x 2in) rectangle and two circles of 6cm (2¼in) and 3cm (1¼in) diameter. Cut out these templates and transfer them to the felt. Cut two large rectangles and one small rectangle from the grey felt, and one circle of each size from the white felt using the zigzag scissors.

2 For the cutlery pouch, place the large circle on one of the large rectangles, roughly in the middle. Starting from the centre of the circle and going through both layers, make a cross (+) using long straight stitches and then an x shape. This will make a lovely star. Add a French knot at the end of each stitch, leaving a small gap.

3 Place a thin line of fabric glue about 1.5cm (¾in) from the top edge, and another one 1.5cm (¾in) from the bottom edge of the felt rectangle. Stick on the ric-rac by pressing it down firmly for a few seconds. Leave about 1cm (½in) of ric-rac sticking out at the sides.

4 Place this grey rectangle on top of the other one, wrong sides together, and sew them together on three sides with a blanket stitch. Leave the top open. Tuck the ends of the ric-rac inside as you stitch for a clean finish.

5 For the napkin ring, place the small circle in the middle of the small rectangle of felt and repeat step 2 for the stitching.

6 Repeat step 3 to attach the ric-rac close to the long edges.

This set looks stylish with a very simple embroidered design. If you are feeling more confident with your embroidery, try stitching a more intricate design or create a unique family monogram.

Colour Clash

Size:
Head circumference 54–58cm (21¼–23in)

Materials:
Schachenmayr SMC Boston or other super-bulky/chunky easy-care yarn in burgundy (132), lavender (47), neon orange (122), fire red (30) and violet/purple (49)

Crochet hook, sizes 7mm (US L/11, UK 2)

Tension sample:
7 sts and 5 rounds of dc (UK tr) using the 7mm (US L/11, UK 2) crochet hook = 10 x 10cm (4 x 4in). Change your hook if necessary to obtain the correct tension (gauge).

Basic pattern:
Work in rounds of dc (UK tr). Start every round with 3 ch, which represents the 1st dc (UK tr), and end every round with a sl st into the 3rd ch from the start of the round.

Changing colours:
Work 1 round each in burgundy, lavender, neon orange, fire red and violet/purple. Repeat the colours in order until the beanie is the desired size.

NB: For the colour change, the new colour should be introduced on the last loop of the previous st to give a perfect colour transition. In this case, the final st of each round is a sl st, which should therefore be worked in the next colour.

Tip:
To save on buying lots of different balls of wool – or if you simply like a plainer style – the hat can be made in just one colour using two balls of yarn, or in two or three colours, using one ball of each.

Instructions:
Start the beanie at the crown and work down to the bottom edge in rounds.

Begin with 3 ch in burgundy then join into a ring with a sl st. Now work as follows:

Round 1 (burgundy): 3 ch, work 11 dc (UK tr) into the ring. Close up this and all subsequent rounds with a sl st in the next colour.

Round 2 (lavender): Work 2 dc (UK tr) into each st around [24 sts].

Round 3 (neon orange): 3 ch, 2 dc (UK tr) into the next st, * 1 dc (UK tr) into the next st then 2 dc (UK tr) into the next st * , rep from * to * around [36 sts].

Round 4 (fire red): 3 ch, 1 dc (UK tr) into each st around [36 sts].

Rounds 5–14: Following the same colour order, work 1 dc (UK tr) into each st around, replacing the 1st dc (UK tr) with 3 ch each time.

Round 15 (violet): 1 ch, sc (UK dc) into each st around then join up the round with a sl st.

Round 16 (burgundy): Work rev sc (UK rev dc) into each st around then fasten off the yarn and darn in the ends. To work rev sc (UK rev dc), simply work from left to right instead of from right to left.

Candy Sugar Bracelet

Materials:

11 x Pandora-style wood beads in various colours, 14 x 8mm (½ x ¼in)

1.7m (68in) of blue 2mm round leather cord

Tools:

Scissors

Instructions:

1 Cut two pieces of leather cord, one approximately 70cm (28in) the other 100cm (40in) long.

2 Take the smaller piece and fold it in half. Pin the fold to a surface. This is your base strand.

3 Tie the longer piece to the base piece just below the fold, leaving a large enough loop to fit over one wood bead. Ensure the two strands of the longer piece are even in length and lie either side of the base strand.

4 Wrap the right-hand strand around the base strand, going over the base strand and then back under. Do the same with the left-hand strand.

5 Now thread a bead on to the right-hand strand, and then thread the left-hand strand through the same bead. The threads will have swapped sides. Pull the strands tight.

6 Wrap the outer strands around the base strand, as you did in step 4.

7 Repeat steps 5 and 6 until you've added all the beads except one.

8 Knot the two longer strands together, then thread all four strands through your remaining wood bead. Knot all the four strands together. Trim any excess threads.

9 To secure the bracelet on your wrist, take the loop from the beginning of the bracelet and hook it over the knot and end bead at the other end.

The Natural Look
*Alter the style of this simple
bracelet dramatically by using
natural-coloured suede cord and
natural wood beads.*

Simple Lace

Materials:

2 x 100g hanks of DK silk
blend wool – variegated
green/blue, 270m (295yd)

Needles:

1 pair of 4.5mm (UK 7; US
7) single-pointed knitting
needles

Large-eyed tapestry needle

Instructions:

Initial rows

Rows 1–2: Using 4.5mm (UK 7; US 7) needles cast on 47 sts in
variegated green/blue, ktbl on return row (i.e. row 2).

Scarf pattern

Row 1: Knit (right side).

Row 2: Purl.

Row 3: (right side) k2, *yfwd, k2tog, k1*, repeat from * to * until
end of row.

Row 4: Purl.

Repeat rows 1–4 until work measures 182cm (71½in).

Cast off sts.

Making up

Sew in loose ends using the tapestry needle.

This scarf will suit all seasons as it is made from a mixture of merino wool and silk. It is made from a very simple lace stitch and the length and width can be adapted to suit your taste.

Key Charm Bracelet

Materials:

Approximately 20cm (7¾in) of brass chain
– 4 links per 3.5cm (1⅜in)

10 brass key charms in varying shapes
and sizes

12 amber and copper cathedral beads

12 head pins

12 brass jump rings – 5mm (³⁄₁₆in)

11 brass jump rings – 7mm (¼in)

Brass lobster clasp
– 8 x 15mm (⁵⁄₁₆ x ⅝in)

Tools:

Flat nose pliers
Round nose pliers

Instructions:

1 Use the flat nose pliers to open one link at one end of the chain. Slip on the lobster clasp and close the link.

2 Measure the length of chain required for your wrist and remove excess links of chain by opening a link and slipping them off. Add a large jump ring to the chain end opposite the lobster clasp.

3 Thread each cathedral bead on to a head pin and use round nose pliers to form a loop with the end securing the bead.

4 Use small jump rings to attach the cathedral beads to the chain and large jump rings to attach the keys. Position the beads and keys in a random fashion along both sides of the chain links.

Hearts and Pearls

Here, the bead caps, decorative pearls and crystal rondelles add a luscious opulence to the various heart charms.

Sunflower Fairy

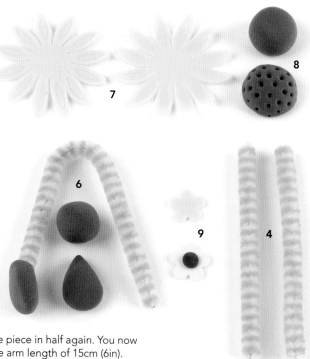

Materials:

60g (2⅛oz) dark green modelling paste

50g (1⅔oz) brown modelling paste or chocolate paste

Small amount of yellow flower/gum paste

Yellow and green striped pipe cleaner

Two white stamens

Cocktail sticks

Tools:

Pointed tool with round end

Smiley tool or drinking straw

Cocktail sticks

Cutters: large daisy, tiny blossom

Thin palette knife

Small pair of scissors

Fine black fibre-tip pen

Sugar glue

Instructions:

1 Make a green body as shown on page 7, insert an 8cm (3¼in) cocktail stick and make two holes in the front for the legs with the pointed tool.

2 For the head, roll a 20g (⅔oz) ball of brown paste into a smooth ball. Support it on a cocktail stick and use a pointed tool to make the holes for the eyes and nose, and the smiley tool for the mouth. Insert two stamens for the eyes and mark the pupils with a fine black fibre-tip pen.

3 Make a nose by rolling a small ball of brown paste into a round-ended cone, then insert it into the hole and secure using a little glue.

4 Cut a pipe cleaner in half and one piece in half again. You now have two legs of 7.5cm (3in) and one arm length of 15cm (6in).

5 For the shoes, roll 12g (⁵⁄₁₂oz) of green paste into a ball then use the scissors to cut it in half to make two flat ovals. Lightly glue both ends of one 7.5cm (3in) length of pipe cleaner, then insert one end into the shoe and the other end into the body. Repeat for the other leg. Bend each pipe cleaner into shape when dry.

6 To make the hands, roll 3g (⅛oz) of brown paste into a ball. Cut the ball in half to make two ovals. Add a little sugar glue to each end of the 15cm (6in) pipe cleaner and attach the hands. Bend the pipe cleaner around the back of the cocktail stick and glue in place, bringing the arms and hands down.

7 Roll out the yellow paste and use the daisy cutter to cut out five flowers. Soften the petal edges with the rounded end of a pointed tool, then, using a little sugar glue, place a flower on top of the pipe cleaner. Repeat with a second flower. Glue the head on firmly and attach three more flowers to the top of the head as shown.

8 Roll a small ball of brown paste into a flat disc and glue it on top of the flowers on the top of the head. Make little holes in the paste with a cocktail stick.

9 Decorate the feet with two tiny blossoms cut from yellow paste with tiny dots of brown paste glued in the centre.

Louise

This sunny character would make an ideal Easter cake topper, or she might make a fun decoration for your window sill.

20 Twenty to Make

A fantastic craft series from Search Press

Pewter Jewellery — Sandy Griffiths

Easy Knitted Tea Cosies — Lee Ann Garrett

Knitted Wrist Warmers — Monica Russel

Sugar Christmas Decorations — Georgie Godbold

Crocheted Beanies

Knitted Beanies — Susie Johns

Bunting and Pennants — Kate Haxell

Knitted Flowers — Susie Johns

Mini Christmas Knits — Sue Stratford

Polymer Clay Buttons — Karen Walker

Fabric Flowers — Kate Haxell

Needle Felties — Susanna Wallis

Knitted Boot Cuffs — Monica Russel

Chocolate Animals — Frances McNaughton

Knitted Phone Sox — Susan Cordes

Knitted Vegetables — Susie Johns

Knitted Fruit — Susie Johns

Wild Women — Stitched Art Brooches

Celebration Cake Pops — Paula MacLeod

Sugar Flowers — Lisa Slatter

All *20 to Make* titles are available as ebooks. Please enquire at head office. UK tel: 01892 510850